just

A LITTLE BOOK OF LIQUID ELEGANCE

MARTINIS.

Cheryl Charming

Photographs by Susan Bourgoin

Lyons Press
Guilford, Connecticut

An imprint of Globe Pequot Press

The following manufacturers/names appearing in *Just Martinis* are trademarks: Absolut®, Absolut® Citron, Absolut® Peppar, Alizé® Red Passion, Angostura®, Bitter Truth Celery Bitters, Campari®, Chambord®, Cointreau®, Curaçao, DeKuyper® Sour Apple Pucker, Fee Brothers, Godiva®, Gordon's®, Green Chartreuse, Hershey®, Jolly Rancher®, Kina Lillet, Lillet Blanc, Meyer, Monin, Noilly Prat®, Peter Heering Cherry Heering, POM Wonderful LLC, Pop Rocks, Rose's®, Smirnoff®, Smirnoff® Ice, St-Germain Elderflower, Van Gogh®

Photo credits: page iv: Shutterstock.com; page vi: Shutterstock.com © drKaczmar; page 12: Shutterstock.com © James Blinn; page 50: Shutterstock.com © SergioZ

Prop Credits:
Bar tools and products provided by www.barproducts.com.
Cocktail sticks, picks, straws, and drink decoration novelties provided by Spirit Foodservice, Inc. (www.spirit foodservice.com).

Text design by Georgiana Goodwin

Library of Congress Cataloging-in-Publication Data
Charming, Cheryl.
  Just martinis : a little book of liquid elegance / Cheryl Charming ; photographs by Susan Bourgoin.
    p. cm.
  Includes index.
  ISBN 978-1-59921-897-7
  1. Martinis. I. Title.
  TX951.C4676 2010
  641.8'74—dc22

                                                              2009043602

Printed in China

10 9 8 7 6 5 4 3 2 1

CONTENTS

The martini is without doubt the king of cocktails.

It's an icon in modern society as well as in the cocktail culture worldwide. Since the mid-1800s, this drink (originally made with gin) has risen and fallen in popularity and has gone through many ingredient changes, but the common denominator has always been its inherent coolness. Some say making a martini is simple, whereas others believe it's an art form.

In 1953, Ian Fleming wrote the first known Vodka Martini into literature. Not only that, it was shaken, not stirred. Bond named the martini after his love interest, Vesper. In 1962, the first James Bond film, *Dr. No*, hit the silver screen showing Bond ordering and shaking a Vodka Martini made with Smirnoff vodka. Vodka was a new spirit to Americans in the 1950s, and they didn't take a liking to it until the debonair James Bond endorsed it.

So, whether you're a vodka or gin lover, the recipes that follow will have you shaking or stirring with confidence. If you're a purist, try the standard Classic Martini or Dirty Martini. Feeling more adventurous? You'll find many modern twists to inspire you ●

Producing the perfect martini, no matter the type or flavor, will require some finesse and equipment on the part of its maker.

Here's a rundown of what you'll need and how you'll use it to mix impressive, tasty martinis.

SHAKERS AND STRAINERS

Every drink maker should know a few ways to strain a martini. Straining is all about keeping ice and other large ingredients out of the cocktail. Ice is an important factor when making a cocktail. Ideally, you should use 1-inch ice cubes. Large ice creates less water dilution and keeps cocktails cold longer.

MIXING GLASS AND BAR SPOON

A mixing glass is a tempered 16-ounce glass. A thick, untempered pint glass can be substituted. Mixing glasses can be used for stirring a cocktail, muddling, and for the other half of a Boston shaker. Use a mixing glass when a recipe calls for stirring instead of shaking. Stirring chills a cocktail without adding air bubbles into the drink, as shaking does.

Bar spoons are long so they can reach the top of tall glasses. Bar spoons have long, spiraled handles. They can be found with a variety of ends, such as the traditional red knob, disc, and even forked. The forked end is used to get olives from a jar.

JULEP STRAINER

The julep strainer is believed to have started as a tea strainer and crossed over to the bar in the late 1800s. The julep strainer is used with mixing glasses so that

you can strain the cocktail without the ice falling into the glass. It fits concave into the glass. The top two drinks that use a julep strainer are the Classic Martini and the Manhattan.

Practice with a glass of ice water to develop the feel for this strainer.

COBBLER SHAKER

The cobbler is the three-piece shaker that you shake and take off the little lid, then strain through the built-in strainer. These shakers became popular during Prohibition. They were produced in many novelty shapes, such as a boot, bullet, or lighthouse.

BOSTON SHAKER

A basic Boston shaker consists of a 16-ounce mixing glass fitted inside a 28-ounce shaker tin. It helps to use a vinyl- or rubber-coated shaker tin so your hands can handle the cold.

Just firmly tap on top of the glass to ensure a tight fit, then shake glass side up for a minimum of ten seconds. To release, hold vertically tin side down,

then firmly tap on the top of the tin on the side of the glass that is not touching.

HAWTHORNE STRAINER

The Hawthorne strainer has a coiled ring that fits inside a shaker tin.

This strainer requires a firm but light touch.

When straining, press firmly inward toward the inside of the tin, not down, or else it will stop the flow of liquid and liquid will seep out the sides.

Hawthorne strainers can be found in a variety of colors, styles, and coatings.

SPECIAL TOUCHES

There's nothing worse than preparing a nicely chilled cocktail, then pouring it into a glass that is warm or room temperature. The temperature of your cocktail immediately begins to rise. Always chill the glass before pouring a strained drink. Also, with the martini craze glasses have become very important. Look for smaller cocktail glasses that are no larger than 7 ounces to keep your cocktail chilly to the bitter end.

Your guests will also be impressed if you take the time to add some professional touches such as layers, garnishes, and colorful decorations.

CHILLING GLASSWARE

You should always prechill a cocktail glass when making a martini. The martini is all about being very cold. You can have glasses ready from the freezer or prechill by putting ice and water into a glass while making the cocktail. Another way to chill is to keep glasses in the freezer. It's also recommended to use smaller vintage-sized glasses (4–6 ounces) to keep the martini cold longer. There's nothing more undesirable than a warm martini halfway down the glass.

LAYERING

Practice layering at home with ingredients from your kitchen such as oils, vinegars, water, and juice. Layering requires a steady hand. You can break the fall of the liquid with practically anything. Most bars use a spoon or cherry. When layering several spirits and liqueurs or several drinks, have all your bottles set in a row and ready to go.

Stylized Layering

Layering takes a bit of practice, but after you get it you got it. An advanced and stylized way to layer is to use a disc-ended bar spoon. The disc end goes into the glass, and you pour the spirit or liqueur on the spiral handle. It travels and spirals down into the glass.

RIMMING

Rimming something on the rim of a glass requires two things: something wet or sticky and your chosen edible ingredient. Saucers and plates work well for holding

your ingredients. Lemon juice mixes well with sugar-based rims, and lime juice mixes well with salted rims.

Strive to rim the outside edge of the glass only. Sugar falling into a Lemon Drop Martini will change the taste of the drink. Flavored rims are meant to complement the flavor of the cocktail and to enhance the taste as it reaches your lips.

Sticking Power

The easiest way to wet the rim of a glass is to take a slice of citrus and rub it around the rim. But sometimes this is not enough sticking power to hold cookie and candy crumbs. You may have to use simple syrup, honey, or even Karo syrup. If you have the time, apply it with a paintbrush.

MAKING TWISTS

A "twist" is a thin strip of lemon rind that is twisted over a cocktail to release its oils, then gently rubbed around the rim of the glass so that the pungent citrus oil can be tasted when taking a drink. The most popular drink that calls for a lemon twist is a Classic Martini (think James Bond). Your guests can choose

not to eat the garnish and set it aside on a cocktail
napkin or push it into the drink.

1. Cut the ends off a lemon.

2. Slip a spoon between the rind and the meat, then
   run it around the lemon on both ends. The goal
   is to separate the meat from the rind. Another
   way is to make a lengthwise slice in the rind, then
   separate the rind and meat with your fingertips or
   spoon.

3. Vertically slice the whole rind once. Or, if you
   prefer, you can lay the rind on its side and make
   one slice. This slice is the lengthwise slice you'd
   be making in the other way using your fingertips
   or spoon. Make sure to save the lemon meat for
   juicing.

4. Tightly roll up the lemon rind.

5. Secure the rolled rind with a bamboo or toothpick
   by pushing it all the way through the rind.
   Securing the rind makes the next step of slicing

easier. Some people don't secure the rind and just hold it tightly with their fingers. It can be done but be warned of its slip factor.

6. Slice the secured rolled rind to make twists. An average lemon can yield up to eight twists. Fatter lemons make for longer twists. Another way to make twists is to cut lengthwise strips around a lemon, then cut off one end. You can now pull off a twist as you need one. However, these will be shorter ●

Gin is the starting point when it comes to traditional martinis (i.e., the pre–James Bond variety).

The main categories of gin are Genever (sweet/malty), London Dry (crisp/dry), Plymouth (fruity/aromatic), and New Western Dry (herbal/flowery).

Vodka provides a blank canvas that allows much experimentation for martini makers, whether dry or sweet. The birth of the Cosmopolitan took place in Miami in 1988 when Absolut released its second flavored vodka, Citron (its first was "Absolut Peppar"). In the mid-1990s, it was available at posh bars and lounges in the big cities, but when Carrie Bradshaw ordered a "Cosmo" on HBO's *Sex in the City*, the floodgates were open for the vodka-based martinis of today.

The Lemon Drop Martini followed the Cosmopolitan as another citrusy girly drink to be shaken, then strained into a seductively sexy cocktail glass. The Appletini hit the trendy wet spots of the world immediately after the Lemon Drop Martini because it was then that sour apple schnapps was introduced. And soon after, the Chocolate-tini made its debut ●

Classic Martini

INGREDIENTS

Ice
2 ounces gin
$\frac{1}{4}$ ounce dry vermouth
2 large olives and/or a lemon twist garnish

1. Chill a 4–6-ounce cocktail glass.

2. Fill a mixing glass half with ice.

3. Pour in the ingredients and stir with ice.

4. Strain into the chilled cocktail glass. Add garnish.

Classic Martinis should always be stirred and never shaken because shaking a cocktail adds air, resulting in a light and bubbly feel on the tongue. In addition, it dilutes much water into the cocktail. Stirring a martini keeps the alcohol smooth and silky, yielding a perfect portion of dilution from the ice. To reach a chilled temperature, stir twenty times clockwise, then twenty times counterclockwise.

Gibson

INGREDIENTS

Ice
2 ounces gin
$1/4$ ounce dry vermouth
Garnish with 2 cocktail onions

1. Chill a 4–6-ounce cocktail glass.

2. Fill a mixing glass half with ice.

3. Pour in the ingredients and stir with ice.

4. Strain into the chilled cocktail glass. Add garnish.

Decoding the Classic Martinis

Dry means having less vermouth.

Extra dry means having no vermouth.

In and out means to swirl the vermouth inside the glass, then dump out the remaining.

Perfect means to use half dry vermouth and half sweet vermouth. As in a Perfect Manhattan.

Mist means to mist a layer of vermouth across the top of the drink with a small atomizer or mister.

Dirty can have many levels of dirtiness depending on how much olive brine is added to the martini.

Dirty Martini

INGREDIENTS

Ice
2 ounces gin
$1/4$ ounce dry vermouth
$1/2$ ounce olive brine
2 large olives and/or a lemon twist garnish

1. Chill a 4–6-ounce cocktail glass.

2. Fill a mixing glass half with ice.

3. Pour in the ingredients and stir with ice.

4. Strain into the chilled cocktail glass. Add garnish.

Of course, you can make a martini in a jelly jar with holes punched in the lid for straining, and you can even use an iced teaspoon to stir! But make it easy for yourself and invest in the proper bar tools needed for making classic martinis. You'll need a mixing glass, julep strainer, and a bar spoon. Using a disc-ended bar spoon works the best.

Nineteen-fourteen

INGREDIENTS

Ice
2 ounces gin
$\frac{1}{2}$ ounce Cointreau
$\frac{1}{2}$ ounce fresh lemon juice
Half an organic egg white

1. Chill a 7-ounce cocktail glass with ice.

2. Shake ingredients with ice.

3. Strain into the chilled cocktail glass.

4. If preferred sweeter, then add more Cointreau.

Believe it or not, America's first distillery was built in the 1640s on Staten Island, and it produced gin. It's hard to believe that it took another two hundred years for the cocktail to be in vogue.

Pegu Club

INGREDIENTS

Ice
1 ounce gin
1 ounce orange Curaçao
¼ ounce fresh lime juice
1 dash each of orange and Angostura bitters
Lime wedge garnish

1. Chill a 7-ounce cocktail glass with ice.

2. Shake ingredients with ice.

3. Strain into the chilled cocktail glass. Add garnish.

The Pegu Club was named after the Rangoon, Burma (Myanmar), gentlemen's club of the same name. Traveling British business gentlemen inspired elite private clubs such as this one so they could have the luxuries of home. The original club no longer stands, but New York City built a Pegu Club in its honor. Inside you can order this cocktail as well as many other vintage cocktails, no matter what your sex.

Gimlet

INGREDIENTS

Ice
2 ounces gin
1 ounce Rose's Lime Juice
Lime garnish

1. Chill a 7-ounce cocktail glass with ice.

2. Shake ingredients with ice.

3. Strain into the chilled cocktail glass. Add garnish.

4. Can be made on the rocks as well.

Gin is one of the spirits that modern mixologists love to experiment with because it embodies many herbs and botanicals and it has been written up in cocktail recipe books since 1862.

Vesper

INGREDIENTS

Ice
2 ounces gin
1 ounce vodka
$\frac{1}{2}$ ounce Lillet Blanc
Lemon twist garnish

1. Chill a 4–6-ounce cocktail glass.

2. Fill a mixing glass half with ice.

3. Pour in the ingredients and stir with ice.

4. Strain into the chilled cocktail glass. Add garnish.

James Bond's exact words in Ian Fleming's novel when ordering a martini are, "Three measures of Gordon's, one of vodka, half a measure of Kina Lillet, shake it very well until it's ice cold, then add a large thin slice of lemon peel. Got it?" The Kina Lillet is extinct, so Lillet Blanc is acceptable in its place.

Vodka Martini

INGREDIENTS

Ice
2 ounces vodka
$1/2$ ounce dry vermouth
2 large olives and/or a lemon twist garnish

1. Chill a 4–6-ounce cocktail glass.

2. Fill a mixing glass half with ice.

3. Pour in the ingredients and stir with ice.

4. Strain into the chilled cocktail glass. Add garnish.

Vodka exploded when James Bond ordered a Vodka Martini, shaken not stirred, in the 1962 film *Dr. No*.

Original Cosmopolitan

INGREDIENTS

Ice
2 ounces Absolut Citron vodka
$\frac{1}{2}$ ounce triple sec
$\frac{1}{2}$ ounce lime cordial
1 ounce cranberry juice
Lime wedge garnish

1. Chill a 7-ounce cocktail glass with ice.

2. Shake ingredients with ice.

3. Strain into the chilled cocktail glass. Add garnish.

THE CLASSICS

Cosmopolitan

INGREDIENTS

Ice
2 ounces citrus vodka
$\frac{1}{2}$ ounce Cointreau
$\frac{1}{2}$ ounce fresh lime juice
1 ounce cranberry juice
Lemon twist garnish

1. Chill a 7-ounce cocktail glass with ice.

2. Shake ingredients with ice.

3. Strain into the chilled cocktail glass. Add garnish.

Rob Roy

INGREDIENTS

Ice
2 ounces blended Scotch whiskey
1 ounce sweet vermouth
2 dashes Angostura bitters
Lemon twist garnish

1. Chill a 4–6-ounce cocktail glass.

2. Fill a mixing glass half with ice.

3. Pour in the ingredients and stir with ice.

4. Strain into the chilled cocktail glass. Add garnish.

Blood and Sand

INGREDIENTS

Ice
1 ounce blended Scotch whiskey
$1/2$ ounce Peter Heering Cherry Heering
$1/2$ ounce sweet vermouth
1 ounce fresh blood orange juice
Lime garnish

1. Chill a 7-ounce cocktail glass with ice.

2. Shake ingredients with ice.

3. Strain into the chilled cocktail glass. Add garnish.

The cocktail Blood and Sand is named after the 1922 bullfighting film of the same name. Rudolph Valentino was the star. He said many times that it was his favorite film. The creator of the cocktail is not known, but the recipe first showed up in print in the 1930 *Savoy Cocktail Book*.

Sidecar

INGREDIENTS

Sugar to rim glass
1 ounce brandy
1 ounce Cointreau
1 ounce fresh lemon juice
Ice

1. Chill a 7-ounce cocktail glass, then rim with sugar.

2. Shake ingredients with ice.

3. Strain into the cocktail glass.

It's strongly believed that Sidecars were served at the spring 1956 wedding of Grace Kelly and Prince Rainier III at the palace of Monaco.

Americano

INGREDIENTS

Ice
1 ounce sweet vermouth
1 ounce Campari
1 ounce soda water
Lemon twist garnish

1. Chill a 7-ounce cocktail glass with ice.

2. Stir ingredients with ice.

3. Strain into the chilled cocktail glass. Add garnish.

4. Can be made on the rocks as well. Some like to add more soda water.

The Americano was first served in Cafe Campari in Milan in the 1860s.

Lemon Drop Martini

INGREDIENTS

Sugar to rim glass
Ice
2 ounces citrus vodka
$\frac{1}{2}$ ounce Cointreau
1 ounce fresh lemon juice
1 ounce simple syrup
Lemon wedge/wheel garnish

1. Rim a chilled cocktail glass with sugar.

2. Shake the ingredients with ice.

3. Strain into the chilled sugar-rimmed glass. Add garnish.

To make the best Lemon Drop Martini, you must use fresh-squeezed lemon juice and simple syrup, not store-bought sweet-and-sour mix. You can purchase simple syrup, but it's better to make your own.

THE CLASSICS

Chocolate-tini

INGREDIENTS

Shredded dark chocolate rim for garnish
Ice
2 ounces vodka
2 ounces white crème de cacao

1. Shred chocolate with a vegetable peeler.

2. Rim a chilled cocktail glass with shredded chocolate.

3. Shake the ingredients with ice.

4. Strain into the chilled chocolate-rimmed glass.

The three base vodkas to use in a Chocolate-tini are a 2-ounce portion of plain, vanilla, or chocolate vodka. If you add another flavored vodka in addition to a base vodka, then you would reduce the portion size to 1 ounce. Flavored vodka choices could be raspberry, strawberry, banana, cherry, coconut, lemon, and orange. Liqueur choices are plentiful. Taking a trip to your local liquor store's liqueur section will spawn a world of possibilities.

Brandy Alexander

INGREDIENTS

Ice
1½ ounces brandy
1½ ounces dark crème de cacao
2 ounces cream
Sprinkle of nutmeg for garnish

1. Chill a 7-ounce cocktail glass with ice.

2. Shake ingredients with ice.

3. Strain into the chilled cocktail glass. Add garnish.

4. Can be made over ice or blended with vanilla ice cream.

The Brandy Alexander was supposedly created for the 1922 arranged royal wedding of Lord Viscount Lascelles and Princess Mary at Westminster Abbey in London. She was twenty-four, and he was forty. This sweet, chocolate brandy cocktail garnished with nutmeg became popular thereafter. It even made it to the first episode of the *Mary Tyler Moore* TV show and is believed to have been John Lennon's favorite cocktail.

Appletini

INGREDIENTS

Ice
1 ounce citrus vodka
1 ounce sour apple schnapps
1 ounce fresh lemon juice
1 ounce simple syrup
Cherry or Granny Smith apple slice garnish

1. Chill a 7-ounce cocktail glass with ice.

2. Shake ingredients with ice.

3. Strain into the chilled cocktail glass. Add garnish.

Garnishes for the Appletini family could include swirling caramel inside the glass or sticking a caramel candy on the rim. And on the wild side, you could drop green apple-flavored jelly beans or hard candy into your drink.

The beautiful thing about martinis is that they lend themselves to many interesting twists.

A basic Chocolate-tini, for example, can be made even more sophisticated with a touch of orange, mint, banana, raspberry, coffee, or pear. In like manner, a simple Cosmopolitan can be transformed into a show-stopping White Raspberry Cosmo. Such decadence!

Speaking of decadence, do you have a favorite dessert or candy? Simply match up the flavors and make a martini. Don't limit yourself to flavored spirits; make sure you look at the many flavors available in the liqueur and mixer aisle as well. Need inspiration? Walk down your local grocery store's candy and cake aisle.

Garnishing a dessert martini can be fun. Add special touches with creative rims made of crushed Oreo cookies, other cookies, sprinkles, and more!

Party martinis (or should we call them "parti-nis"?) should be fun, whether it's the color, garnish, flavor, or name of the drink. Your goal when present-ing party drinks to guests is to see a look of excite-ment on their faces. When you see that look, then you know you've succeeded ●

White Raspberry Cosmo

INGREDIENTS

Ice
$^3/_4$ ounce raspberry vodka
$^3/_4$ ounce citrus vodka
$^3/_4$ ounce Cointreau
$^1/_2$ ounce fresh lime juice
2 ounces white cranberry juice
Raspberry garnish

1. Chill a cocktail glass with ice.

2. Shake all the ingredients with ice.

3. Strain into the glass. Add garnish.

> The big twist on the Cosmo is using white cranberry juice in place of red cranberry juice. To bump up the flavor factor, we added raspberry vodka. You can also try other flavored vodkas such as strawberry, grape, mango, mandarin, and orange.

MODERN VARIATIONS

Fountain of Youth

INGREDIENTS

Filtered ice
2 ounces organic black cherry–infused organic
   vodka
1 ounce açaí juice
1/2 ounce aloe juice
1 ounce POM Wonderful cherry juice
1 ounce organic lemon juice
3 ounces organic sparkling pear cider
Organic cherry garnish

1. Shake all the ingredients (except the organic
   pear cider) with filtered ice.

2. Strain into a large stemmed glass.

3. Top with organic pear cider. Add garnish.

Açaí (pronounced ah-SIGH-ee) berry juice is
the latest antioxidant phenomenon. It is found
on palm trees along the Amazon River and,
as you guessed, contains ingredients to cure
whatever ails you. However, most intriguing
are studies that show a slowing of the aging
process. So açaí berry juice wins the title of
best fountain of youth juice.

Kama Sutra

INGREDIENTS

Sugar to rim glass
Ice
1 ounce cherry vodka
1 ounce Alizé Red Passion liqueur
1 ounce fresh lemon juice
2 ounces Smirnoff Ice
Cherry garnish

1. Rim a cocktail glass with sugar.

2. Shake the first three ingredients with ice.

3. Strain into the glass.

4. Top with Smirnoff Ice. Add garnish.

> The Kama Sutra is made with cherry vodka, but that can easily be replaced with raspberry or strawberry vodka if that suits your taste buds. The most important ingredient is the lemon juice because you need the citrus to balance out the sweetness of the sugar rim. The Alizé is available in two flavors and colors; make sure you get the Red Passion flavor.

Dusk

INGREDIENTS

Ice
½ ounce pear vodka
1 ounce St-Germain elderflower liqueur
1 ounce crème de violette
1 ounce fresh Meyer lemon juice

1. Chill a 4–6-ounce cocktail glass with ice.

2. Stir all ingredients with ice.

3. Strain into a cocktail glass.

When the sun is 6 degrees below the horizon, it produces dreamy colors across the evening sky. This time of day is called "dusk." The Dusk cocktail looks like one of those colors. The crème de violette was extinct for many years but has now been resurrected thanks to modern bartender efforts.

Gypsy Bloodless Mary

INGREDIENTS

Ice
2 ounces cucumber-infused gin
$\frac{1}{2}$ ounce Noilly Prat French dry vermouth
2 dashes The Bitter Truth Celery Bitters
Celery salt rim and cucumber or celery garnish

1. Chill a 4-6-ounce cocktail glass with ice, then rim with celery salt.

2. Stir all ingredients with ice.

3. Strain into the cocktail glass. Add garnish.

The Gypsy Bloodless Mary is a great example of a marriage between fresh ideas and historic ingredients. The original Bloody Mary was made with gin, and this modern cocktail is a little twist on this tomato-based libation . . . without the tomato. Noilly Prat French dry vermouth has been handcrafted in the south of France in the small village of Marseillan on the Mediterranean coast since 1813.

Tainted Virtue

INGREDIENTS

Ice

1$\frac{1}{2}$ ounces Madagascar vanilla bean–infused
   vodka

$\frac{1}{2}$ ounce Drambuie

$\frac{1}{2}$ ounce raw simple syrup

1 ounce cold espresso

2 ounces fresh cream garnish

1. Chill a 4–6-ounce cocktail glass with ice.

2. Shake all ingredients with ice.

3. Strain into the cocktail glass.

Raspberry Lemon Drop Martini

INGREDIENTS

Sugar to rim glass
Ice
1 ounce citrus vodka
1 ounce raspberry vodka
$\frac{1}{2}$ ounce Chambord
1 ounce fresh lemon juice
1 ounce simple syrup
Lemon wedge/wheel garnish

1. Rim a chilled cocktail glass with sugar.

2. Shake the ingredients with ice.

3. Strain into the chilled sugar-rimmed glass. Add garnish.

Blueberry Lemon Drop Martini

INGREDIENTS

Blue-colored sugar to rim glass (see page 68)
Ice
1 ounce citrus vodka
1 ounce blueberry vodka
1/2 ounce Cointreau
1 ounce fresh lemon juice
1 ounce simple syrup
Lemon wheel and 3 blueberries for garnish

1. Rim a chilled cocktail glass with sugar.

2. Shake the ingredients with ice.

3. Strain into the chilled blue sugar–rimmed glass. Add garnish.

Every lemon yields different amounts of juice, so always squeeze with a hand juicer or other juicer, then measure out the portion you need. You'll get the most juice from a heavy room-temperature lemon. Simply roll the lemon with your palm on the countertop to break up the juice inside, cut in half, then squeeze. Strain through a sieve or mesh strainer to remove the seeds and pulp.

Banana Drop Martini

INGREDIENTS

Yellow-colored sugar to rim glass
Ice
1 ounce citrus vodka
1 ounce banana vodka
$\frac{1}{2}$ ounce Cointreau
1 ounce fresh lemon juice
1 ounce simple syrup
Lemon wheel garnish

1. Rim a chilled cocktail glass with sugar.

2. Shake the ingredients with ice.

3. Strain into the chilled yellow sugar-rimmed glass. Add garnish.

To bump up the fun a bit, use different colors and types of sugars to rim your Lemon Drop Martinis. You can make colored sugar by putting sugar and a few drops of food coloring into a jar or plastic bag, then shaking. Try the new neon colors available in the spice aisle at your local grocery store, too!

Oz

INGREDIENTS

Ice

1½ ounces rose petal and blue poppy seed–
   infused premium orange vodka

1 ounce Green Chartreuse

1 ounce fresh Meyer lemon juice

1 mist of rose water

1. Chill a 4-6-ounce cocktail glass with ice.

2. Shake all ingredients with ice except the rose water.

3. Strain into a cocktail glass.

4. Spray a mist of rose water across the top of the drink.

The Oz gets its name from the Green Chartreuse, whose color is reminiscent of the Emerald City. Green Chartreuse is a liqueur that is made from 130 herbs. It has been made by monks since 1605 and was finally perfected in 1764. Fans of Chartreuse include Bon Jovi, the Smithereens, and the late Queen Elizabeth Bowes-Lyon. It was also mentioned in the novel *The Great Gatsby* (1925) and seen in the film *Grindhouse* (2007).

White Chocolate-tini

INGREDIENTS

Chocolate syrup garnish
Ice
1 ounce vanilla vodka
$\frac{1}{2}$ ounce white crème de cacao
$\frac{1}{2}$ ounce Godiva white chocolate liqueur
1 ounce half-and-half

1. Rim a chilled cocktail glass with chocolate syrup.

2. Shake the ingredients with ice.

3. Strain into the chocolate syrup–rimmed glass.

> You can rim a glass with cocoa powder, powdered hot chocolate mix, shredded chocolate, and so forth. The inside of the glass can be coated in chocolate syrups, and the garnishes can range from the many choices of chocolate candy available, bite-sized chocolate cakes, brownies, cookies, and more!

Strawberry Chocolate-tini

INGREDIENTS

Chocolate and strawberry syrup
Chocolate-dipped strawberry for garnish
Ice
1 ounce vanilla vodka
1 ounce strawberry vodka
1 ounce white crème de cacao
1 ounce half-and-half

1. Crisscross the syrups into a cocktail glass.

2. Shake the ingredients with ice.

3. Strain into the chocolate and strawberry syrup cocktail glass.

Transfer the syrup from the clunky, plastic, store-bought bottles into some condiment squirt bottles, such as those used at picnics for ketchup or mustard. The mouth will be much smaller, allowing you lots of control to make any design. When making many drinks for a party, set the glasses on waxed paper and swirl or crisscross your heart out.

Pink Chocolate-tini

INGREDIENTS

Shaved chocolate to rim glass
2 ounces vanilla vodka
1½ ounces white crème de cacao
¼ ounce grenadine

1. Rim a cocktail glass with shaved chocolate.

2. Shake all the ingredients with ice.

3. Strain into the glass.

Don't be afraid of using a drop of food coloring in place of the grenadine in the Chocolate-tini. A rainbow of colors can be used!

Skinny Chocolate-tini

INGREDIENTS

Ice
2 ounces vanilla vodka
1 ounce Monin sugar-free chocolate syrup
2 ounces half-and-half
Crushed sugar-free Oreo to rim glass

1. Rim a cocktail glass with crushed sugar-free Oreos.

2. Shake all the ingredients with ice.

3. Strain into the glass.

> Dip rim in the sugar-free syrup first so that cookie crumbs will stick.

Box of Chocolates

INGREDIENTS

Chocolate syrup for swirl
Ice
1 ounce vanilla vodka
1 ounce butterscotch schnapps
1 ounce Irish Cream
1 ounce half-and-half
Chocolate candy garnish

1. Swirl chocolate into cocktail glass.

2. Shake the ingredients with ice.

3. Strain into the glass. Add garnish.

Richard Cadbury introduced the Valentine's Day box of chocolates in 1868. So, why not put it to use and garnish a special cocktail for Valentine's Day?

Message Martini

INGREDIENTS

Chocolate syrup
Ice
2 ounces chocolate vodka
2 ounces white chocolate liqueur
1 ounce half-and-half

1. Write message inside a cocktail glass with chilled chocolate syrup.

2. Shake the ingredients with ice.

3. Slowly strain into the glass.

- Transfer chocolate syrup to condiment bottles and chill for better control.
- You can also paint with chocolate using a small paintbrush.
- Place glasses in freezer to set before pouring drink.
- Remember that you'll have to write words backward.
- Little tubes of cake frosting work well, too. Just make sure that you strain the drink into the glass very slowly so as not to disturb your message.

MODERN VARIATIONS

Washington Appletini

INGREDIENTS

Ice
1 ounce whiskey
1 ounce sour apple schnapps
2 ounces cranberry juice

1. Chill a 7-ounce cocktail glass with ice.

2. Shake ingredients with ice.

3. Strain into the chilled cocktail glass.

Caramel Appletini

INGREDIENTS

Caramel syrup
Ice
1 ounce apple vodka
1 ounce sour apple schnapps
1 ounce butterscotch schnapps
1 ounce fresh lemon juice
1 ounce simple syrup
Green apple slice garnish

1. Swirl caramel into a cocktail glass.

2. Shake ingredients with ice.

3. Strain into the cocktail glass. Add garnish.

Jolly Rancher candy got its name from the Golden, Colorado, company owners, Bill and Dorothy Harmsen. They felt that the name has a friendly, western sound. Today Hershey owns the candy. For fun you can make your own green apple-flavored vodka. Drop ten green apple Jolly Ranchers into your favorite vodka overnight, and it'll be ready the next morning.

Pucker Up

INGREDIENTS

Ice
1 ounce sour apple vodka
1 ounce watermelon pucker schnapps
1 ounce lime juice
Wax lips garnish

1. Chill a cocktail glass with ice.

2. Shake the ingredients with ice.

3. Strain into the glass. Add garnish.

Not only was DeKuyper's Sour Apple Pucker the first sour apple schnapps, but it's also the reason why the word Appletini is in our modern vocabulary. If you like sour flavors, get ready to pucker up!

Forbidden Appletini

INGREDIENTS

Ice
2 ounces citrus vodka
2 ounces sour apple schnapps
Green apple slice and gummy worm garnish

1. Chill a cocktail glass with ice.

2. Shake all the ingredients with ice.

3. Strain into the glass. Add garnish.

To keep apple slices fresh, soak them in lemon water or a product made for this task.

Pineapple Upside-down Cake

INGREDIENTS

1 ounce vanilla vodka
1 ounce Irish Cream
2 ounces pineapple juice
Ice
$\frac{1}{2}$ ounce grenadine
Pineapple ring, whipped cream, and a cherry
  garnish

1. Shake the ingredients except for the grenadine and pineapple ring.

2. Shake ingredients with ice.

3. Strain into the chilled cocktail glass.

4. Pour in the grenadine, and it will sink to the bottom. Add garnish.

MODERN VARIATIONS

You can easily make many nonalcoholic dessert martini versions using flavored extracts from the spice section of your local grocer. There is also an incredible choice of syrup flavors. You'll find an assortment of exotic and unique flavors such as kiwi, huckleberry, pumpkin, tiramisu, and lemongrass. Sugarfree varieties are available, too!

Almond Joy-tini

INGREDIENTS

Chocolate syrup and shredded coconut garnish
Ice
1 ounce vanilla vodka
1 ounce crème de cacao
1 ounce coconut rum
1 ounce half-and-half

1. Rim a cocktail glass with chocolate syrup and coconut flakes.

2. Shake ingredients with ice.

3. Strain into the chilled cocktail glass.

Try this with your other favorite candy bars! To determine what portions to match up to a candy bar, for example, simply look at the ingredients on the package. The ingredients are always listed from the largest portion to the least.

MODERN VARIATIONS

Key Lime Pie-tini

INGREDIENTS

Graham cracker crumbs to rim glass
Ice
2 ounces lime vodka
1 ounce simple syrup
$\frac{1}{2}$ ounce lime cordial
1 ounce half-and-half
Whipped cream and lime garnish

1. Rim a cocktail glass with graham cracker crumbs.

2. Shake ingredients with ice.

3. Strain into the chilled cocktail glass. Add garnish.

> Have you ever squirted whipped cream into a drink, and it flopped over? That's because the liquid doesn't provide stability. The trick is to anchor the whipped cream to the side of the glass. You'll find this tip especially helpful for hot drinks because the heat adds to the melting process. The Pineapple Upside-down Cake's stability comes from the pineapple.

Winter Wonderland

INGREDIENTS

Ice
2 ounces coconut rum
1 ounce white crème de cacao
Dash blue Curaçao
Coconut-vanilla ice-cream ball garnish

1. Chill a cocktail glass with ice.

2. Shake all the ingredients with ice.

3. Strain into the glass. Add garnish.

To make the coconut-vanilla snowballs ahead of time, gather these items: two cookie pans, vanilla ice cream, shredded white coconut, and rubber gloves. Place one cookie pan in the freezer, then pour the coconut onto the other pan. In assembly-line fashion, put on the gloves, scoop some ice cream, form it into a ball, then roll in the coconut. Place on the tray in the freezer and keep working until you make the amount of snowballs needed.

Candy Cane

INGREDIENTS

Crushed candy cane to rim glass
Ice
2 ounces vanilla vodka
1 ounce peppermint schnapps or white crème
de menthe

1. Rim a cocktail glass with crushed peppermint candy.

2. Shake all the ingredients with ice.

3. Strain into the glass.

If you don't feel like crushing peppermint candy in your grinder or banging at it in a plastic bag, then make it easy on yourself and just drop one candy into the cocktail. You can even use a candy cane as a garnish. Take one look down the candy aisle, and you'll come up with lots of ideas.

Flirtini

INGREDIENTS

$1/2$ ounce vodka
1 ounce pineapple juice
4 ounces Champagne

1. Pour the vodka and juice into a Champagne glass.

2. Pour in the Champagne.

The Flirtini is from the TV show *Sex and the City*. It is mentioned at a New York City rooftop party when Samantha asks Carrie what she's drinking. Today you can twist it up by using pineapple vodka. One thing you don't want to do is shake and strain the vodka and pineapple juice first because the pineapple juice is too frothy.

MODERN VARIATIONS

Tickled Pink

INGREDIENTS

Pink sugar to rim glass
Organic rose petals
5 ounces raspberry vodka
$\frac{1}{2}$ ounce lemon juice
$\frac{1}{2}$ ounce rose syrup
5 ounces brut rosé Champagne

1. Rim a Champagne glass with pink sugar. Then drop in rose petals.

2. Shake the next three ingredients with ice.

3. Strain into a Champagne glass.

4. Pour in the Champagne.

Radical Raspberry Sidecar

INGREDIENTS

Raw organic sugar to rim glass
Filtered ice
2 ounces organic cognac
$\frac{1}{2}$ ounce Monin organic raspberry syrup (or
   from scratch)
1 ounce organic lemon juice

1. Rim a cocktail glass with organic raw sugar.

2. Shake all the ingredients with filtered ice.

3. Strain into the glass.

As for the Radical Raspberry Sidecar, know
you're not limited to that flavor. Look in the
produce section at other fruits you can use
for syrup or puree. The best flavor choices are
strawberries, blackberries, blueberries, and
peaches. Or you can leave the flavor out alto-
gether, substituting organic raw simple syrup.

Berry Scary-tini

INGREDIENTS

Black sugar to rim glass
Ice
3/4 ounce black vodka
3/4 ounce blueberry vodka
1 ounce raspberry liqueur
2 ounces lemon juice
Raspberry garnish

1. Rim a cocktail glass with black sugar.

2. Shake all the ingredients with ice.

3. Strain into the glass. Add garnish.

Liquid black food coloring became common on shelves in 2007. You can find it at your local grocer in the spice section. If you can't find black vodka, then make your own! Simply put three drops of food coloring into a 750-milliliter bottle of vodka (or any other spirit, for that matter). Other black choices can be found at candy and cake supply stores.

Ultraviolet

INGREDIENTS

Purple sugar and edible purple glitter to rim
  glass
2 ounces Van Gogh açaí-blueberry vodka
1/4 ounce Chambord raspberry liqueur
1 ounce lemon juice

1. Rim a cocktail glass with the purple sugar
   mixture.

2. Shake all the ingredients with ice.

3. Strain into the glass.

Basic drink rims consist of coarse salt or sugar.
Salt can be colored or mixed with a variety of
flavors such as chili powder, cracked espresso
beans, citrus zest, and ginger. Sugar can be
colored or flavored with spices such as cin-
namon, or you can use cake sprinkles, hot
chocolate powder, and any crushed candy
imaginable such as red hots or lemonheads.

  Other choices include crushed nuts,
shaved chocolate, frosted chopped cherries,
shredded coconut, crushed cookies, or edible
metallics.

Pop Star

INGREDIENTS

Strawberry Pop Rocks to rim glass
Ice
2 ounces green apple vodka
2 ounces strawberry pucker schnapps
1 ounce lemon juice
Star fruit slice garnish

1. Rim a cocktail glass with the strawberry Pop Rocks.

2. Shake all the ingredients with ice.

3. Strain into the glass. Add garnish.

Crush rimmed ingredients by putting them into a plastic bag and gently hitting with a heavy object. The ingredient chosen to stick your rimmed ingredients to the glass will require different sticking power. Salt and sugar rims can be rubbed with citrus or dipped into liquor or liqueurs. Cookies, coconut, and anything chunky requires something stickier like Karo syrup, chocolate syrup, or honey.

Yin Yang-tini

INGREDIENTS

Ice
2 ounces vanilla vodka
2 ounces dark crème de cacao
1 ounce hazelnut liqueur
1 ounce half-and-half
Shredded white chocolate and chocolate discs

1. Cut half of a yin-yang template from cardboard based on the size of your chosen glass.

2. Blend all the ingredients with half a cup of ice.

3. Pour into the glass.

4. Place the cardboard template over half of the top of the glass and sprinkle shredded white chocolate. Place the chocolate discs on top of the drink.

Simple syrup is simply sugar and water mixed together to make a liquid sugar.

Sugar in syrup form is the ideal way to add sweetness to a cocktail. Granulated sugar doesn't dissolve as well.

For the simple syrup recipe, a ratio of 1:1 works fine, but some people prefer it a little thicker and will use twice as much sugar as is called for in this recipe. You'll discover your preference after you begin to experiment. For the water, try to use the highest quality available, and for sugar you have choices of raw, organic, brown, and more.

To make infused simple syrup, you simply add clean herbs, fruits, veggies, spices, and so forth to the water. Bring it to a boil, add the sugar, and stir until the sugar is dissolved. Remove from the heat, cover, and allow it to cool and steep. After about 30 minutes you can strain and funnel into a jar or bottle. Simple syrup will keep in the fridge for a month.

For a no-heat sugar-free simple syrup, use filtered room-temperature water and shake it hard with Splenda in a jar or bottle. You'll notice that the Splenda dissolves very quickly. Simply refrigerate ●

Simple Syrup

INGREDIENTS

2 cups water
2 cups sugar

1. Bring the water to a boil.

2. Pour in the sugar. Stir until dissolved.

3. Remove from heat and allow cooling.

4. Funnel into a jar or bottle.

Simple Syrup Tips
- Sterilize all jars and bottles to be used.
- Wash hands thoroughly.
- Try to buy organic and always wash and always rinse your infusion ingredients well.
- If you do not have filtered water, then boil water twice to purify.

Tri-Citrus Infused Simple Syrup

INGREDIENTS

2 cups water
Zest from 1 lime, 1 lemon, and 1 orange
2 cups sugar

1. Bring the water and the citrus zest to a boil.

2. Pour in the sugar. Stir until dissolved.

3. Remove from heat and allow to cool and steep for 30 minutes.

4. Strain and funnel into a jar or bottle.

No-Heat Simple Syrup

INGREDIENTS

2 cups sugar
2 cups lukewarm water

1. Funnel the sugar and water into a bottle.

2. Seal cap and shake hard for 10 seconds.

3. Let sit for 1 minute, then shake hard again until sugar is dissolved. Cloudiness will clear.

To infuse spirits, all you need are alcohol, your chosen infusion ingredients, a wide-mouthed jar, and time.

Simply pour the spirit into a sterilized wide-mouthed jar, add the washed and rinsed edible infusion of choice, and seal the top. Set the jar in a cabinet and every day turn it upside down once and back, then set it back in the cabinet. After a few days, you can open the jar and taste-test it.

Stronger flavors that take only three to four days include vanilla, mint, and citrus rinds. Edibles that take up to a week include pitted cherries, apples, raspberries, peaches, strawberries, blueberries, and mangos. Fibrous edibles like chiles take up to two weeks. If you combine flavors, then you may not be able to put them in at the same time ●

Vanilla-infused Vodka

INGREDIENTS

1 750-milliliter bottle premium vodka
3 vanilla beans cut and scraped

1. Pour the vodka into a sterile, wide-mouthed jar.

2. Add vanilla pods. Seal jar.

3. Set in a dark cool place and agitate once daily for four days.

4. Strain and funnel into a sterile jar or bottle.

BAR AND DRINK SUPPLIES

Barproducts.com
www.barproducts.com

Every bar tool featured in this book came from bar products.com. It has been selling bar supplies since 1995 and is the official supply store for *Nightclub and Bar* magazine.

Fee Brothers
www.feebrothers.com

Fee Brothers is a four-generation-old (since 1863) manufacturer of top-quality cocktail mixes, bitters, and flavoring syrups. Look here first when searching for an unusual ingredient like assorted bitters, falernum, gomme, and orgeat.

LeNell's Ltd.
www.lenells.com

This wine and spirit boutique specializes in hard-to-find spirits, so if you see an ingredient in this book that you cannot find at your local liquor store, try LeNell's.

Spirit Foodservice, Inc.

www.spiritfoodservice.com

Spirit Foodservice, Inc. makes custom and specialty drink stirrers, specialty straws, novelty cocktail picks, and other goodies for your drinks. It has been around since 1934 ●

Some bars and lounges merely serve drinks.

Other establishments serve liquid delights worthy of the gods. Here's a list of some we found that are dedicated to the craft of the cocktail.

CALIFORNIA: SAN FRANCISCO

Absinthe Brasserie and Bar

www.absinthe.com

398 Hayes St.

(415) 551-1590

Absinthe Brasserie and Bar is one of the most romantic and popular fine-dining establishments in San Francisco, serving classic and creative upscale American-influenced French brasserie as well as an extensive handcrafted cocktail menu.

Bourbon & Branch

www.bourbonandbranch.com

501 Jones St.

(Phone number and password are gained only by registering online for a reservation.)

Bourbon & Branch is a throwback to the 1920s and the era of Prohibition when the sale and consumption of alcoholic beverages were outlawed. You'll experience the ambience of that time in an actual speakeasy that operated illegally at its location from 1921 to 1933. There are rules here: Do not use a cell phone, smoke only out back, do not stand at the bar, and be patient for labor-intensive cocktails.

Cantina

www.cantinasf.com

580 Sutter St.

(415) 398-0195

Cantina is a Latin abode, an art salon, and a culinary cocktail lounge featuring wines and spirits shaken and poured in nouveau ways. Owned by master mixologist Duggan McDonnell.

Elixir

www.elixirsf.com

16th and Guerrero

(415) 552-1633

The first certified green bar in San Francisco, Elixir has an expansive cocktail menu and a spirits collection that focuses on the vintage, the organic, the local, and the original, all while remaining a friendly corner bar. Owned by H. Joseph Ehrmann.

Forbidden Island Tiki Lounge

www.forbiddenislandalameda.com

1304 Lincoln Ave.

(510) 749-0332

Forbidden Island Tiki Lounge serves vintage tropical drinks and modern cocktails made perfectly balanced with fresh-squeezed, seasonal juices and premium ingredients.

FLORIDA: FORT LAUDERDALE

Mai-Kai

www.maikai.com

3599 N. Federal Highway (U.S. 1)

(954) 563-3272

The Mai-Kai is the sole survivor of America's grand midcentury tiki supper clubs; its stellar tiki cocktails, food, and decor provide an experience unmatched for anyone.

FLORIDA: SOUTH BEACH/MIAMI

The Florida Room
www.delano-hotel.com
Delano Hotel
1685 Collins
(305) 672-2000
The Florida Room is an intimate speakeasy that evokes a bygone era and serves handcrafted specialty cocktails imbued with a Cuban/Latin feel. The room has a Lucite grand piano that has been played by music legends such as Lenny Kravitz and Jamie Foxx.

LOUISIANA: NEW ORLEANS

Arnaud's French 75 Bar
www.arnauds.com/bar.html
813 Rue Beinville
(504) 523-5433

The French 75 Bar has been in Arnaud's since 1918. The crafted drink menu is extensive, with drinks ranging from the cocktail for which the bar is named to a dizzying selection of martinis and other cocktails.

Carousel Bar

www.hotelmonteleone.com

Monteleone Hotel

214 Rue Royale

(504) 523-3341

The Carousel Bar is immortalized in the writings of Ernest Hemingway and others. The historic bar top and stools take you on a slow, fifteen-minute ride around the bar.

Swizzle Stick Bar

www.swizzlestickbar.com

Loews New Orleans Hotel

300 Poydras St.

(504) 595-3305

The Swizzle Stick Bar was inspired by the famous Brennans' beloved Aunt Adelaide, who personified the avant-garde cocktail culture of the late 1950s and

1960s, and represents the joie de vivre of all that is
New Orleans.

NEW YORK: NEW YORK CITY

Death + Company

www.deathandcompany.com

433 East 6th St.

(212) 388-0882

Death + Company is a restaurant/bar that celebrates
the golden age of the cocktail of days gone by and
of today. The crafted cocktail menu is extensive. No
reservations. First come, first served.

Flatiron Lounge

www.flatironlounge.com

37 W. 19th St.

(212) 727-7741

Flatiron Lounge is co-owned by bar chef Julie Reiner.
She draws much of her inspiration from her native
Hawaii by utilizing the freshest fruits and the highest-
quality spices and spirits available.

PDT

www.pdtnyc.com

113 St. Mark's Place

(212) 614-0386

PDT (Please Don't Tell) is a modern, Prohibition-
era speakeasy serving crafted cocktails. Some on the
menu, such as bacon-infused bourbon, are extreme.
The entrance is not seen from the street, and there is
no sign. The front door is located inside an adjacent
store (Crif Dogs hot dogs) and is camouflaged as
a phone booth. Once inside the booth, you lift the
receiver, hit the call button, and wait for the person
on the other side to let you in.

Milk & Honey

www.mlkhny.com/newyork

134 Eldridge St.

The tiny Milk & Honey bar is a true speakeasy
that has a constantly changing phone number and
requires a password for admission. There is no visible
entrance, and everything is freshly made, from the ice
to the bitters. The owner, Sasha Petraske, created the

bar in personal retaliation against celebrity-obsessed nightlife. Only nonfamous folk receive the unlisted phone numbers and must call ahead to be buzzed in through the surveillance system–equipped door.

Pegu Club

www.peguclub.com

77 West Houston St., 2nd Floor

(212) 473-PEGU

Pegu Club was opened by cocktail goddess Audrey Saunders and bar chef Julie Reiner. Located in Manhattan's Soho district, it is revered by cocktail enthusiasts as one of the best cocktail lounges in the world. The name pays tribute to a storied, late-nineteenth-century British officers club in Burma (Myanmar), which has since closed.

OREGON: PORTLAND

Mint/820

www.mintand820.com

816 North Russell

(503) 284-5518

Mint/820 is owned by Lucy Brennan. Lucy is at the forefront of creating cocktails that incorporate fresh fruit and food into each drink and has been noted as one of the top mixologists in the country by *Food and Wine* and *Bon Appetit* magazines.

Teardrop Lounge
www.teardroplounge.com
1015 NW Everett St.
(503) 445-8109
This lounge offers lovingly made libations with crafted mixers, tinctures, specialty liqueurs in liquid culinary style.

WASHINGTON: SEATTLE

Zig Zag Café
www.zigzagcafe.net
1501 Western Ave.
(206) 625-1146
The award-winning Zig Zag Café was born from the desire to provide its patrons with an unprecedented selection of the finest spirits. One bartender, Murray

Stenson, is widely revered and universally beloved. Murray has been serving cocktails in Seattle for over thirty years, inspiring scores of cocktail aficionados and fellow bartenders along the way ●